C**O**MPASS
True Stories for Kids

Broken Pieces

An Orphan of the Halifax Explosion

Allison Lawlor

N**IMBUS**
PUBLISHING

Nimbus Publishing Limited
3731 Mackintosh St, Halifax, NS B3K 5A5
(902) 455-4286 nimbus.ca

Printed and bound in Canada

NB1235

Design: Jenn Embree

Library and Archives Canada Cataloguing in Publication

Lawlor, Allison, 1971-, author
Broken pieces : an orphan of the Halifax explosion / Allison Lawlor.
(Compass : true stories for kids)
Includes bibliographical references and index.
ISBN 978-1-77108-515-1 (softcover)

1. Halifax Explosion, Halifax, N.S., 1917—Juvenile literature.
2. Halifax Explosion, Halifax, N.S., 1917—Pictorial works—Juvenile literature. I. Title. II. Series: Compass (Halifax, N.S.)

FC2346.4.L39 2017   j971.6'22503   C2017-904097-9

Nimbus Publishing acknowledges the financial support for its publishing activities from the Government of Canada, the Canada Council for the Arts, and from the Province of Nova Scotia. We are pleased to work in partnership with the Province of Nova Scotia to develop and promote our creative industries for the benefit of all Nova Scotians.

Contents

The SS *Mont Blanc,* the French cargo ship carrying explosives that collided with the SS *Imo,* causing the Halifax Explosion.

The SS *Imo* was a Norwegian ship carrying relief supplies at the time of the explosion.

Introduction

More than one hundred years ago, there was a huge boom in Halifax that was so loud and so terrifying that one man who heard it thought it meant the world was ending.

Luckily, he was wrong. It wasn't the end of the world. What the man heard was the sound of a ship exploding in the Halifax Harbour—a disaster that sent 3,121 tons of iron and steel pieces flying for kilometres, destroying nearly everything in their path.

Looking back, it is easy to see how the disaster could have been avoided. But sadly, it did happen. On December 6, 1917, at four minutes and thirty-five seconds after nine o'clock in the morning, two big ships, the steamship **SS** *Imo* from Norway and the freighter **SS** *Mont Blanc* from France, carrying lots of explosives, hit each other in Halifax Harbour. A fire on board the *Mont Blanc* caused its cargo to ignite, leading to what would become known as the Halifax Explosion.

In an instant, church steeples collapsed, ships and

Front page of the *Halifax Herald* on December 7, 1917.

trains were thrown into the air as though tossed like toys. Beautiful, tall maple trees snapped in two and every window for kilometres shattered into tiny pieces. Hundreds of people were blinded when sharp glass from the windows flew into their eyes. Even hundreds of kilometres away on Cape Breton Island, dishes were reported to have rattled in cupboards and dogs barked as the hair on their necks stood straight up—a signal that

Broken Pieces

The Halifax City Hall clock stopped at 9:05 from the force of the explosion.

something scary was taking place.

The power of the blast even caused a **tsunami**—a huge, forceful wave—that rose from the harbour and destroyed nearly everything along the shores of Halifax and Dartmouth. The explosion killed over 1,900 people, and 9,000 people were injured by fires, flying glass, or collapsing buildings. Many were trapped under fallen buildings and houses while fires raged all around them.

At the moment of the explosion, just before 9:05 in the morning, the hands on the City Hall clock in the centre of Halifax stopped. City officials decided to never fix it. The hands on the clock remind us to never forget the explosion, but also prompt us to ask questions and to learn why it happened. If we do that, maybe we can prevent another tragedy like this from ever happening again.

WARTIME HALIFAX

When people living in and around Halifax woke up on December 6, 1917, they might have thought it was going to be just another ordinary day. But it wasn't. In December 1917, the world was at war. The First World War had started three years earlier in Europe. In Halifax, there wasn't any fighting, but the city was filled with **enlisted** men coming and going overseas, and there was fear everywhere. People were afraid Germany would attack. If the world hadn't been at war in 1917, the Halifax Explosion would never have happened.

It was the war that brought the Norwegian ship *Imo* and the French freighter *Mont Blanc* into Halifax Harbour. If the world hadn't been at war, the *Mont Blanc* wouldn't have been filled with explosives and the worst human-made disaster in the world's history wouldn't have happened. (The explosion remained the biggest until August 6, 1945, when the atom bomb was dropped on Hiroshima, Japan, during the Second World War.)

But out of the disaster came remarkable stories of bravery, kindness, and hope. People came together to help however they could. Often with nothing more than their hands, they provided assistance by carrying an injured person to the hospital or digging a child out from under a fallen house.

Immediately after the explosion, help came from across the country and around the world. Soldiers and sailors who were in Halifax waiting to be shipped overseas were not only available to rescue people, but were also trained to respond to emergencies.

In the days after the explosion, Halifax newspapers were filled with the names of missing people and those thought to be dead. There were also notices from parents and other relatives desperately hoping to find their lost family members.

Barbara Orr was one of the thousands of children whose lives were devastated by the explosion.

Barbara Orr, who was born on March 4, 1903, lived in the Richmond neighbourhood in Halifax's North End, and survived the explosion. Because it was located so close to the harbour, Richmond was one of the hardest-hit neighbourhoods in the city. Barbara, who was fourteen years old at the time, suffered serious injuries that left her unable to walk for months. She was lucky to be alive, but in the days after the explosion she didn't know whether or not her family had been killed.

Reading about the explosion today seems otherworldly—like it could only happen in a science fiction book or in a faraway country, not a safe place like Halifax. But life in 1917 wasn't as safe as it is today, and was in general more difficult. In Halifax, houses didn't have telephones or electrical lights. People relied on candles or kerosene lamps to see in the dark. They didn't have cars, so they walked to get places in the city or relied on horses pulling carts for transportation. If they had to travel farther away, they took the train. When they got sick, there weren't as many medicines, so more people died from diseases that are easily treated today.

Many people who study history see the Halifax Explosion as an important moment not only for Nova Scotia, but for Canada. The explosion brought the horrors of war close to home for many Canadians. Before the explosion, the war seemed far away on the battlefields in Europe. But in a moment, the explosion destroyed Barbara's community, making it look like a battlefield in France.

Broken Pieces

The destruction permanently changed the landscape of Halifax and Dartmouth. Many of the city's old buildings fell to the ground and lots of the buildings that stand today were constructed during the months after the explosion.

But before we learn more about the Halifax Explosion and its aftermath, let's see what life was like in the Halifax area one hundred years ago.

The view of Halifax from Fort Needham, c. 1780.

CHAPTER 1:

Life in Halifax in 1917

For fourteen-year-old Barbara Orr and her five younger brothers and sisters, living in Halifax's North-End community of Richmond was exciting. It was a bustling part of the city filled with businesses, schools, and homes surrounding a big hill that extended up from the harbour.

From the water, the ground rose steeply to the top of a 66-metre hill to a place known as Fort Needham. The fort had been used in the past to defend the city and its naval dockyards from the enemy, dating back to the American Revolution more than 240 years earlier.

RICHMOND

By 1917, the area surrounding Fort Needham had a busy dockyard, wharves, and factories. One of the factories was the Acadia Sugar Refinery where many men worked, and another was the Richmond Printing

Company on Barrington Street where Barbara's father, Samuel, worked. He was also one of the owners. Inside the large building made of granite blocks, men and women worked at heavy printing presses, which were used to make things like newspapers and books. Barbara's uncle, William, was one of the printers.

Barbara's father could walk to work from the Orr's white, wooden house on the corner of Kenny and Albert Streets. The Orrs were a big family. There was Samuel; his wife, Annie; Barbara, whose red hair was usually worn in two braids and reminded people of Anne Shirley from the book *Anne of Green Gables*; Ian, age twelve; Mary, age ten; Archibald (Archie), age nine; Isabel, age six; and James, age three.

Most of the homes in Richmond were made of wood and were heated by stoves that burned wood in winter. Only some had electricity. Many had indoor bathrooms that included a toilet, but some did not, and people used outhouses. Some of the families who lived in Richmond were poor and lived in run-down houses, but most lived in working-class apartments or middle-class homes. Most families didn't have a car.

Living in Richmond was like living in the country because many families had a cow for milk and chickens for

In 1749, led by Edward Cornwallis, ships carrying about two thousand five hundred British settlers arrived and eventually established a town called Halifax. It became the capital of Nova Scotia and the leading port city on Canada's east coast. It was a good location because it was closest to Europe. Halifax continued to grow as ships carrying wood and fish and other goods sailed in and out of the city's harbour.

fresh eggs. There were berry bushes all around and in the summer the children picked blueberries and blackberries.

There were many churches and schools in the area, including Richmond School, which Barbara attended. At that time, where you went to school depended on your family's religious beliefs. The Catholic children in the area went to St. Joseph's School, where most of the teachers were nuns. If you were Protestant like Barbara, you attended Richmond School, which had 421 students divided into seven classrooms. At that time, it was normal to have 60 or more students in one class. Barbara was in grade eight at the time of the explosion. Her teacher, Mr. Huggins, was also the school principal. He taught not only Barbara's grade eight class, but also grades seven and nine.

Life in Halifax in 1917

When Barbara wasn't at school, she and her siblings liked to watch the ships in the harbour from their large front window. Most of the ships were either coming from or going to Europe. There was always movement and excitement. Looking out the window was like watching a movie on a giant screen.

THE HALIFAX HARBOUR

Halifax has one of the best natural harbours in the world. It is connected to Bedford Basin, which is a large sheltered body of water. Joined by a narrow channel of

Halifax has one of the deepest and largest natural harbours in the world.

water called "the Narrows," the harbour and the basin make a shape like an hourglass.

The harbour is a big part of the city's history. For hundreds of years the Mi'kmaq, the area's Indigenous people, lived along its shores. In the early 1600s, explorers from France sailed across the Atlantic Ocean to Nova Scotia.

The First World War, which began in 1914, brought a lot of people, ships, and activity to Halifax. Everywhere you looked there were soldiers in uniform. Many were in Halifax to protect the port in case Germans attacked. Others were being trained at McNabs Island, York Redoubt,

Turtle Grove, also known as Tufts Cove, was a small Mi'kmaw community along the Dartmouth side of the harbour. Fewer than twenty families lived there in 1917, but the community dated back at least to the late 1700s. The community was badly damaged by the explosion, and was never rebuilt.

Wellington Barracks, and the Halifax Armoury while they waited for ships to take them to fight in Europe.

By April 1917, more than fifteen thousand troops had left Halifax by sea—a huge number of people for a city that had a wartime population of about sixty thousand. Today Halifax is much bigger and home to almost four hundred thousand people.

Throughout 1917, Halifax Harbour was crowded with wartime shipping. Nearly two thousand vessels were reported to have passed through the harbour that year. There were so many different kinds of ships for the children to watch: big passenger ships carrying soldiers; cargo ships loaded with food, grain, and horses; supply ships carrying things like weapons, uniforms, and tents needed to fight the war in Europe. Even hospital ships came to Halifax bringing back soldiers who had lost arms, legs, or even their eyesight on the battlefield.

Barbara and her brothers and sisters especially loved to watch the **convoys** of ships that gathered in the Bedford Basin, ready to make the trip across the ocean to Europe.

Broken Pieces

THE FIRST WORLD WAR

The battles in France were so long and fought so hard, that as many as forty or fifty ships loaded with military equipment and ammunition had to be shipped to France every two weeks. Ships filled with guns and ammunition coming from the United States frequently stopped in Halifax on their way to Europe.

Halifax was an important gathering point. German submarines, called U-boats, were a dangerous threat to ships carrying soldiers and supplies. To protect themselves,

The First World War

The First World War was a major conflict fought between 1914 and 1918. Some other names for it are: World War One, WWI, the War to End All Wars, and the Great War.

It might help to think of the beginning of the war as Europe splitting into two families of countries: the Allies and the Central Powers. The Allies were made up of Britain and its empire, as well as France, Belgium, Russia, and later the United States. They were considered part of one family, fighting against the Central Powers: Germany, Austria, Hungary, Bulgaria, and Turkey.

On August 4, 1914, Germany invaded Belgium. Britain had to stick up for Belgium so it declared war on Germany. Since Canada was then a colony of Great Britain and thus one of the Allies, it entered the war at this time too.

Life in Halifax in 1917

navy ships used a convoy system. Merchant ships, which carried supplies, were placed into large groups and escorted across the ocean with warships. A group of thirty or more ships would join together in the basin loaded with food, guns and ammunition, and troops. When they were ready to leave, they would pass, one after the other, through the Narrows and into the main harbour. There they would meet an escort of heavily armed destroyers and fast gunboats, which would travel with them to Europe. These ships would act as their bodyguard.

Before the First World War, ships carrying dangerous cargo such as explosives were not allowed to enter the Halifax Harbour. Since the harbour was so close to businesses, houses, and people, government officials considered it too dangerous to have explosives so close. Instead, ships had to stay outside the harbour, tied up at wharves or quays. But during the war, even dangerous ships were allowed into the harbour because it was sheltered and safe; the wharves outside the harbour were considered "easy targets" for the enemy.

German submarines often tried to come close to Halifax during the First World War. Those who lived in the city were constantly afraid of a German attack.

In 1917, Halifax was crowded with soldiers, including the 1st Regiment Canadian Garrison Artillery. In this photo, they are at Fort Charlotte on Georges Island in the Halifax Harbour.

Two anti-submarine nets stretched across Halifax's harbour to protect its entrance. The nets had gates in them that were opened at different times of day so other ships could come and go, but were always closed at night.

When the *Mont Blanc* arrived off the mouth of Halifax Harbour on December 5, it was late in the afternoon, so the submarine nets were closed. It was too late in the day to enter the harbour, so the ship went to seek shelter by McNabs Island, which was located at the entrance of

Life in Halifax in 1917

The docks in Richmond were busy. Ships and factories, such as the Acadia Sugar Refinery, where the smoke is coming from, filled the area.

the harbour. While the *Mont Blanc* didn't have the extra safety of being inside the harbour, the ship's captain believed it would be safe for the night. He had no idea of the disaster that would happen the next day.

No other disaster in recent history could have prepared the people of Halifax for the tragedy that was to come. Five years earlier, disaster struck close to the city, and people were called to help. In 1912, the famous *Titanic* ship sunk in the North Atlantic Ocean. The people of Halifax helped by recovering hundreds of dead bodies. This time, the city would have to respond to a call for help from its own people.

Life in Halifax in 1917

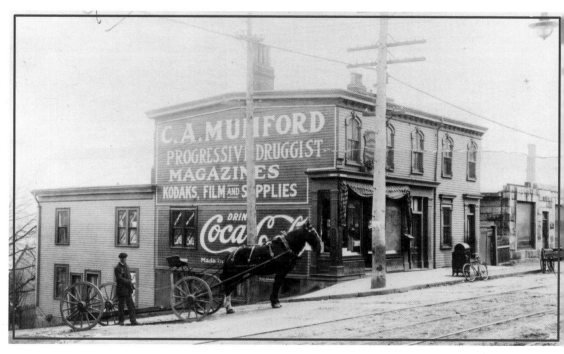

A drug store and the Richmond Printing Company before the explosion.

CHAPTER 2:

Days Before the Explosion

The day before the explosion, Barbara and her siblings were at home. They hadn't gone to school because Archie, Barbara's younger brother, was sick with whooping cough. The whole family was under quarantine for ten days. Being in quarantine meant you weren't allowed to be around other people for fear that you would spread your infection.

In 1917, many children got sick and stayed home from school for long periods of time during the winter. Unlike today, children didn't get vaccinations against diseases and the medicines that were available weren't as good as they are today; they only helped a little, but didn't cure illnesses. Diseases like mumps, measles, chicken pox, and serious infections like scarlet fever and diphtheria were much more common.

Being the oldest child in the family, Barbara would read to her siblings and play games with them when they were home from school. She also helped her mother around the house a lot by cooking and baking and doing other household chores.

Barbara loved school and couldn't wait to get back. Since it was December, she wanted to be there so she could go to choir rehearsal and play practice for the upcoming Christmas concert. All of the Orr children were eager to return to school the following week, as Archie was the only child sick in their family.

On December 5, the harbour was busy as usual. A convoy of ships was getting ready to sail across the Atlantic Ocean. Two of the ships were being loaded with supplies at the Richmond piers not far from Barbara's house. She watched from the big front window as horses and wheat, which would be turned into flour to make bread, were loaded onto the ships. It was hard for her to imagine that in Europe, some of those horses would pull carts full of supplies for soldiers in the battlefields. Others would be used as transportation for soldiers.

THE SS *IMO*

The *Imo* had been in the Bedford Basin for three days. The Belgian Relief Commission was using the old, four-masted steamship to deliver aid, such as food and blankets, to people in Belgium, a country near France. The *Imo* had steamed all the way to Halifax from Rotterdam in the Netherlands.

The ship was different from many of the others in the harbour because it had the words "Belgian Relief" clearly printed in large red letters on its side. This was to let the enemy know that it shouldn't attack the ship because it was not carrying soldiers or ammunition. The sign was supposed to stop German submarines from sinking it.

After getting more fuel in Halifax, the *Imo*'s captain, Haakon From, planned to take the ship to New York where he would pick up food, clothing, and life-saving supplies to bring back to Belgium. People in Belgium badly needed help, but because of the fighting it was hard to get supplies in Europe. They relied on help from countries like Canada and the United States.

The day before the explosion, the *Imo* was ready to leave Halifax but the boat that brought the coal it needed to run its steam engine had arrived late. By the time the coal was

Days Before the Explosion

loaded onto the *Imo*, darkness was setting in. Travelling through the harbour and out to the open ocean late at night was too dangerous.

The gates in the anti-submarine nets, which stretched across the harbour, had already been closed for the night. The *Imo* couldn't pass through them. Buoys on top of the water and concrete weights attached to the bottom of the mesh held the nets in place on the harbour floor. In the morning, the gates would be lifted and the *Imo* would be able to leave. Until then, it would have to wait in the Bedford Basin.

THE SS *MONT BLANC*

Late in the afternoon on that same day, the French ship *Mont Blanc* arrived near Halifax Harbour looking to meet a convoy that would protect it on its return trip to France. It had just travelled to Halifax from New York City. The 3,121-ton freighter was almost twenty years old and tired-looking from having crossed the Atlantic Ocean many times. The ship's captain, Aimé Le Medec, a short French-speaking man with a neatly trimmed black beard, and his crew of almost forty men anchored for the night near McNabs

Island. They were happy to have found shelter. They would wait until the next morning to enter Halifax Harbour.

In New York City, the *Mont Blanc* had been refitted so it could carry much-needed cargo back to France. After the ship was fixed up, stevedores (workers responsible for loading and unloading a ship's cargo) had spent more than a day loading the ship with a deadly mixture of explosives and fuel. The *Mont Blanc* would take these across the ocean to soldiers.

The stevedores in New York had known they were dealing with very dangerous material. They didn't smoke near the ship in case a spark or cigarette ignited an explosion.

They wore cloth over their metal-studded boots when they worked on the ship to prevent the metal nails in the bottoms of their boots from creating sparks as they walked across the ship's decks. They made sure to place the barrels, kegs, and cases of dangerously explosive materials and fuel carefully onto the ship.

On its way from New York City to Halifax, the *Mont Blanc* moved slowly under the weight of so many crates and barrels. The ship couldn't keep up with a small convoy that was leaving New York to cross the ocean to Europe. Since it was too dangerous for the *Mont Blanc* to

An anti-submarine net was stretched across the harbour to protect the ships.

cross the ocean alone, the ship headed to Halifax, where it hoped to find a larger convoy to travel with.

When the *Mont Blanc* arrived in Halifax, a harbour official boarded the ship and inspected its cargo and papers. The cargo listed on the *Mont Blanc* totalled 2,653,115 kilograms. There were 2,146,830 kilograms of wet and dry **picric acid**, a type of explosive; 226,797 kilograms of **TNT**, a dangerous explosive also known as Trinitrotoluene; 56,301 kilograms of **guncotton**, also used as an explosive; and 223,188 kilograms of **benzene**, a liquid that easily lights on fire and is part of gasoline. The ship had the makings of a giant bomb.

But on the night before the Halifax Explosion, few thought of the *Mont Blanc* as a bomb that could potentially explode. That night it was just another ship

Broken Pieces

waiting by the closed entrance to Halifax Harbour for the anti-submarine gates to open in the early morning. The *Mont Blanc's* captain, Aimé Le Medec, could breathe a sigh of relief. He had made it safely to Halifax. Now, he could rest and focus on the ship's safe return to France. That night the Halifax Harbour posed no danger.

The trains travelled along the tracks beside Halifax Harbour. They ran past the Narrows and around the Bedford Basin.

CHAPTER 3:

The Explosion

"When I was a boy and I would see scary things in the news, my mother would say to me: "Look for the helpers. You will always find people who are helping."

—MISTER FRED ROGERS, AMERICAN TELEVISION PERSONALITY—

On December 6, 1917, Barbara woke up and looked outside. It was a bright, cold morning, but there was no snow on the ground. A light wind was in the air, coming from the northwest. Nothing she saw gave her any sign of the disaster that was to come.

In the calm waters of the harbour below Barbara's house, as many as one hundred ships waited for the day's activity to begin. The ferry travelled back and forth between Dartmouth and Halifax, just like it did every day. It was a big ferry that carried not only people, but horses too.

Everything seemed to be just as it always was. The soldiers in the city were doing their usual training activities. People were on their way to work. Children were getting ready to walk to school. At the nearby North Street train station, the morning trains were arriving.

Barbara and her siblings were still in quarantine so they didn't have to get ready for school. Even if it had been a school day for her, she would have been able to sleep in a little. At the beginning of December, schools in Richmond started their winter schedule, which meant classes started at nine-thirty instead of nine o'clock.

THE HOURS BEFORE THE EXPLOSION

At seven-thirty in the morning, the gate in the submarine net at the entrance to the Halifax Harbour opened to allow boats in. The French munitions ship *Mont Blanc* left its spot near McNabs Island and made its way up the Narrows—the narrowest part of the waterway between the basin and the harbour—to the Bedford Basin, which was crowded with ships waiting to join convoys.

Around the same time, the relief ship *Imo* left the Bedford Basin and headed for the Narrows. As the *Imo*

Broken Pieces

approached the Narrows, it increased its speed to almost seven knots. The harbour speed limit was five knots. Having had to wait for coal for the ship's boilers, Captain Haakon From was behind schedule and anxious to get to sea.

At about twenty minutes before nine o'clock, Barbara waved goodbye to her father, who left home to walk the short distance to his workplace. Barbara stood with her brother Ian at the window in their house overlooking the harbour. Ian was the ship expert in the Orr family and liked to tell them about the different vessels entering and exiting. They were used to seeing a busy harbour, so at first they weren't concerned to see the *Mont Blanc* making its way toward the Narrows. The *Mont Blanc* was following the rules for the harbour and stayed to the **starboard**, or right, side. This was the side closest to Dartmouth. Just like when people drive cars and have to follow rules on the road, captains of ships have to follow certain rules to avoid running into each other.

According to the rules, ships heading out of the harbour toward the Atlantic Ocean—like the *Imo* was— were supposed to stay on the **port**, or left, side of the harbour, which was closest to Halifax. Captain Le Medec aboard the *Mont Blanc* was surprised to look ahead and

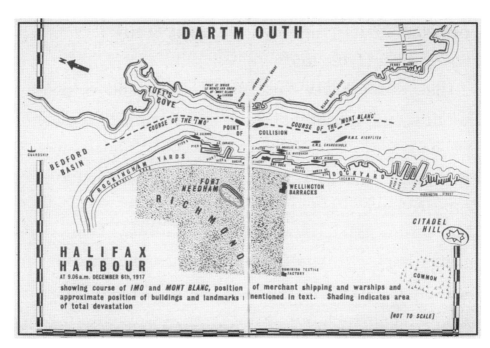

A map of Halifax Harbour in 1917, showing the course of the ships involved in the explosion.

see the *Imo* on the Dartmouth side, instead of the proper Halifax side. It was heading straight at him.

"It looked as if they were trying to run into each other," Barbara later said about the two ships.

The *Mont Blanc* blew its whistle once—a signal to say it was on the correct side of the harbour and would stay on its path. The *Mont Blanc* expected the *Imo* to move over to the Halifax side of the harbour to make room for both ships to pass through the Narrows. But it didn't.

Broken Pieces

The *Imo* blew its whistle twice in reply to say: *I am staying where I am, too.*

The two ships blew their whistles back and forth. At that time, ships didn't have radios on-board like today, which made it more difficult to exchange information. Every captain had to understand what certain whistle patterns meant.

At almost the last minute, the *Mont Blanc* turned to the left, toward Halifax, and the *Imo* reversed its engines to try and move backwards and out of the way of the *Mont Blanc*. But the *Imo* was unable to reverse quickly enough. Its **bow** swung toward the *Mont Blanc*.

THE COLLISION

If only one of the ships hadn't made the move it did, the collision could have been avoided. But the combination of their last-minute efforts made running into each other unavoidable. The *Imo* crashed against the bow of the *Mont Blanc* at about seventeen minutes before nine o'clock in the morning.

The two steel hulls hitting each other caused sparks to fly. On the *Mont Blanc*, the barrels holding the benzene

Vincent Coleman, Dispatcher and Hero

Only a few metres away from the harbour, Vincent Coleman was working at the busy Richmond railway station. Unlike the passenger railway station on North Street made of brick, the Richmond station was much smaller and made of wood. It was situated right in the middle of the rail yard, where all trains arriving in and leaving Halifax passed through.

As a dispatcher, Vincent's job was to control the rail traffic. It wasn't easy because it was always so busy. He had to send orders to the trains that came carrying freight for the ships in the harbour, and tell them whether to wait their turn or proceed. He also had to make sure the passenger trains passed North Street Station, and he routed the hospital trains and trains filled with soldiers from the Pier 2 oceanliner terminal.

On the morning of December 6, Vincent knew train number ten, an overnight express from Saint John, New Brunswick, was scheduled to arrive in Halifax at 9:00 A.M., but it was running ten minutes late. When Vincent saw the fire in the harbour, he knew it was something dangerous. His instinct was confirmed when a sailor ran into his tiny rail station to warn him about the pending explosion.

Vincent was ready to leave the station and run for safety with everyone else, but then he remembered the train heading for Halifax with three hundred innocent people on-board. Someone had to warn the train to stop before it reached the city. Vincent decided to send a **telegram** to the train—the last message he would ever send. Sadly, there wasn't enough time for him to send the message and escape before the explosion. Vincent's final telegram reached the approaching train in time and its conductor was able to stop the train a few kilometres outside of Halifax. When the *Mont Blanc* exploded, the train's cars were pushed off the rails and its windows shattered, but the passengers survived. By sending the message, Vincent not only saved the people onboard the train, but he alerted other communities in Nova Scotia about the tragedy. If he hadn't sent the message, it may have been hours before anyone outside Halifax knew about the disaster. It could have taken much longer for help to arrive. Newspapers later printed different variations on the exact wording of Vincent's message, but the heroic nature of the message never changed. It read something like this: *"Hold up the train. Ammunition ship afire in harbor making for Pier 6 and will explode. Guess this will be my last message. Good-bye boys."*

Broken Pieces

split open, spilling the fuel. The sparks met the benzene and a fire broke out, spreading very quickly throughout the ship. The fire grew bigger and bigger.

Knowing the *Mont Blanc* would blow up once the fire found the explosives in the ship's cargo hold, Captain Le Medec ordered his crew to lower two lifeboats into the harbour and row as fast as they could

Vincent Coleman, a dispatcher at the Richmond railway station, who became a hero.

to the Dartmouth shore. The crew followed orders and abandoned ship. Since they were all from France, no one on-board spoke English. When the crew began shouting warnings about the explosives on the ship, no one understood what they were saying. The unmanned *Imo* drifted toward the Dartmouth shore.

By 8:45 A.M., only minutes after the collision, the *Mont Blanc* was a ball of fire on the water. The burning ship

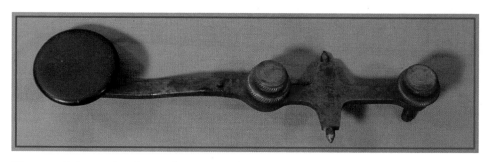

Vincent Coleman's telegraph, now at the Maritime Museum of the Atlantic in Halifax.

drifted closer and closer to the Halifax shore, up to Pier 6 in Richmond. Thick clouds of greyish-black smoke rose into the still morning air. Flames, which looked like orange fireworks, poked up through the smoke.

On the Halifax side, in Barbara's neighbourhood of Richmond, people were unaware of the deadly explosives aboard the *Mont Blanc*. Hundreds of people flocked to their windows and rooftops and ran out into the streets or to the top of Fort Needham to watch the spectacular fire. Barbara and her brother Ian and sister Isabel asked their mother if they could go outside to get a better look. Seeing no danger, their mother said yes. The three siblings left the house while their mother and the three youngest children stayed at home. Ian and Isabel headed straight for the harbour. Barbara stopped by a friend's house to see if she wanted to come along too.

FIRE IN THE HARBOUR

A few minutes later, Constant Upham, who owned a grocery store nearby, called the fire department. He was one of the only people in the area who had a telephone. He knew something wasn't right as he watched the fire in the harbour grow bigger. The West End Fire House sent the Patricia, Halifax's first and only motorized engine, to help. At that time, fire engines were usually pulled by horses. Firefighter William Wells quickly drove the Patricia to Pier 6, right by where the collision had occured, only to find it was now on fire. William wanted to put out the flames and save the pier.

The Patricia was the Halifax Fire Department's first and only motorized fire engine.

Help was also on the way in the harbour. The Royal Canadian Navy and the British Royal Navy sent crews from the HMCS *Niobe* and HMS *Highflyer* in small boats to investigate the fire. Already close to the scene, the tugboat *Stella Maris* used its fire hose to try to stop the flames on the burning ship. But the flames were too big and the little stream of water made no difference. The ship kept burning. Men from the tugboat and navy officers tried towing the *Mont Blanc* away from Pier 6 so it would be further away from houses and people. But after two difficult and dangerous attempts, they had to stop.

THE EXPLOSION

Just before 9:05 A.M. the *Mont Blanc*, which had continued to drift closer to Pier 6 on the Halifax side, exploded in a huge cloud of melting metal. Like an erupting volcano that covers everything in its path with hot lava, or an earthquake that causes every building to crumble with its vibrations, the explosion destroyed all of Richmond. People were crushed and trapped when their homes and workplaces collapsed.

Broken Pieces

Wood stoves were pushed over and uncontrollable fires started everywhere.

The force of the explosion threw the *Mont Blanc*'s anchor—which weighed about 1,200 pounds, about the same amount as an adult male polar bear—through the air and all the way to the Northwest Arm, three whole kilometres away from the harbour.

A clock badly damaged in the explosion.

The explosion also created a tsunami. Within minutes of the explosion, a huge wave more than twelve metres high rolled out of the Halifax Harbour and pushed up Needham Hill. Then, gravity pulled the water back toward the harbour, bringing people and broken buildings with it. The tsunami also swept the *Imo* clear across the harbour, leaving it in the shallow water on the Dartmouth shore. A brief, spooky silence followed the explosion as an oily black cloud hung over the city and pieces of red-hot metal rained down.

Barbara later deescribed the explosion to writer Janet Kitz: "It was so still, so calm, and this terrible, awful

The North Street Railway Station shown after the explosion.

column of smoke went up, and then balls of fire would roll up through it. Then they burst—but there was no sound. It was the strangest thing. I stood spellbound in the middle of this field, and then thought, *oh, something awful is going to happen*," Barbara later said. "Suddenly the explosion went off. I was thinking that I was [falling] down deep holes all the time."

One moment, Barbara was watching the burning ship in the harbour; the next she found herself on the ground on Needham Hill, more than a half kilometre away. It was probably the wave and the force of the explosion

Broken Pieces

that blew her there. One of her legs was caught between two big rocks. They kept her there when the wave moved back down the hill, bringing everything with it.

DEVASTATION

When she woke up, Barbara didn't move at first. She lay still for a few minutes. When she finally sat up, she noticed that one of her boots, which had been tightly laced around her ankle, was gone. Her foot had been badly crushed. She had cuts all over her body and she was covered in oil and dirt from the exploding ship.

Not far away, her two-storey wooden school was destroyed. Richmond School was only about half a kilometre

A huge cloud of smoke rose into the air after the explosion.

Richmond School on Roome Street was wrecked in the Halifax Explosion.

in a straight line away from where the *Mont Blanc* blew up. Two children had been inside the school at the time and they died immediately. Since school didn't start until 9:30 A.M. that morning, most of the children had still been at home or on their way to school. More than eighty of Barbara's schoolmates died that morning.

Schools were usually sturdier buildings than houses. Perhaps if more children had been in classes in other schools further away from the harbour that morning, they might have been better protected. But not at the Richmond School, which was completely destroyed.

Barbara, though badly shaken, was lucky to be alive. Now that she was awake, her one thought was to find her

Broken Pieces

family. In pain from her injuries, she tried desperately to crawl back to the top of Fort Needham. All around, she could see that her entire neighbourhood was on fire—houses, stores, churches, and schools. There was no way she could reach her street through all the smoke and flames.

What was she going to do?

American relief workers, who provided help after the explosion, outside a Halifax hospital.

CHAPTER 4:

Help Arrives

*E*verywhere Barbara looked she saw people who were hurt and bleeding. They looked sad and confused and scared. Many people were so covered in soot and ash from the explosion that their skin was black, as though they had been working in a coal mine all day. People were crying and wandering around as if they were in a bad dream. They didn't know what had happened and they were frightened.

There was panic. Barbara heard someone say: "It's the Germans! The Germans are here!" Many people believed that because of the war, the German enemy had attacked Halifax and caused the explosion. Barbara tried to tell them it wasn't the Germans but a ship that had caught fire and exploded, but none of the grown-ups seemed to hear or believe her.

Unable to reach her house due to the smoke and flames, Barbara made her way slowly to the nearest road.

Turtle Grove (Tufts Cove)

Turtle Grove, also known as Tufts Cove, was a small Mi'kmaw community along the Dartmouth shore of the Halifax Harbour. Fewer than twenty families lived there in 1917, but for hundreds, maybe thousands of years, the Mi'kmaq had lived along the harbour's shores. The community dated back at least to the late 1700s.

Like Richmond, Turtle Grove suffered the full force of the explosion and the tsunami that followed. The recovery of nine bodies is recorded, but more people may have died. Newspapers and historians at the time wrote little about, and didn't pay much attention to, the complete destruction of the Mi'kmaw community.

In the early 1900s, the community at Turtle Grove lived in wigwams, which were birchbark-covered dwellings. Factories and industrialization was pushing the Mi'kmaq out of the area. By 1917, the government was moving ahead with its plan to force Mi'kmaw communities onto reserves (areas of land set aside specifically for First Nation people). Only one month before the explosion, an order had come to move the Turtle Grove community to a location several kilometres away.

After the explosion, the Turtle Grove settlement was never rebuilt.

She didn't know it at the time, but her family's home was one of the 1,630 destroyed that day, either by the explosion or the many fires that quickly spread following the blast.

When Barbara crawled up Fort Needham and reached the road, she found a horse-drawn wagon passing by. It had been turned into a makeshift ambulance. It was taking injured people to the Camp Hill Hospital, a newly built military hospital in the centre of the city. Normally the wagon was used to deliver fresh fish to homes in the

Broken Pieces

The front page article in the *Morning Chronicle*, Halifax, December 10, 1917.

neighbourhood, including Barbara's.

Barbara was helped on to the wagon. She lay, barely moving, with the other badly hurt people. As the wagon moved slowly along the road, Barbara watched as the world, which had suddenly become scary and unrecognizable, passed her by. Everything she was familiar with—her house, her school, the Richmond

Printing Company where her father worked—was no longer there. Left in their place were wrecked buildings and injured, dazed people who were frantically searching for their families, friends, and what was left of their homes.

What these scared and hurt people didn't know was that help was on its way. An American ship called USS *Old Colony*, which was already at the dry dock in Halifax waiting for repairs, miraculously survived the explosion. Within fifteen minutes of the blast, it sent doctors and kits filled with emergency supplies out to help, and the ship itself was turned into a temporary hospital. The US Coast Guard patrol vessel *Morrill*, which was anchored in the Dartmouth Cove waiting for supplies, also sent people and supplies to shore to help.

On land, people organized groups to start searching through the fallen houses and buildings. They looked for those who were trapped or injured, and dug out the bodies of those who had died.

By four o'clock in the afternoon on the day of the explosion, Halifax's fire department had the fires in Richmond under control. Twelve hours later, the fires were mostly out, except in a few isolated areas where the debris continued to burn for several days.

AMERICAN RESPONSE

News of the explosion reached the United States quickly. In the state of Massachusetts, Governor Samuel McCall organized a relief train to leave city of Boston at 10:00 P.M. on the night of the explosion. The train was filled with doctors and nurses and supplies. The train also carried one thousand pillows, thousands of bandages, and medicine to help wounded people.

On the way to Halifax, the train got stuck in a terrible storm. A huge snowdrift covered the track and the train had to stop. It took several men one hour to shovel away the snow before the train could start moving again and eventually reach Halifax.

In the state of New York, a second train filled with supplies also left for Halifax. It was loaded with food, five hundred fold-up beds, eighteen thousand coats and other warm winter clothing, ten thousand blankets, twenty cases of disinfectant, one hundred and sixty cases of supplies doctors would need to perform surgeries, and even more nurses and doctors.

In the days following the explosion, more doctors and nurses would arrive in Halifax from the United States. Help also poured in from all over Canada and

A dog named Jacky

One happy story involved a dog named Jacky. The little brown dog was trapped in an office at the North Street Railway Station during the explosion, but wasn't hurt. The day after the explosion, he found a way out of the collapsed building. Covered in soot from the blast, he ran straight home where he found his family. They were so happy to see him.

other parts of the world. The Massachusetts Eye and Ear Infirmary sent four nurses specifically trained in treating eye and ear injuries to help with the hundreds of people who were deafened by the blast or blinded by flying glass. Almost every window in Halifax and Dartmouth was broken in the explosion. Doctors had to remove more than two hundred and fifty eyes. Dozens of people were left completely blind.

In total, 222 doctors and 459 nurses would arrive in the city within days of the explosion to help care for thousands of injured people.

Many animals were also lost, injured, or left homeless after the explosion. The Society for the Prevention of Cruelty to Animals (SPCA) in Massachusetts sent a thousand American dollars to buy food and to help find homes for animals.

Broken Pieces

WHAT HAPPENED TO THE CHILDREN?

Shortly after the explosion, a special committee was formed to help all the children who had been hurt or who had lost parents. It also helped families search for lost children and repair schools and daycare centres. Seventy children were orphaned in the disaster, hundreds needed serious treatment in hospital, several were blinded, and almost fifty suffered serious eye injuries. At least three hundred children had either their mother or father die in the explosion.

If an orphaned child had relatives who lived nearby, he or she would be sent to live with them. But many children didn't have relatives to care for them. These children went to live in orphanages or were adopted by other families. After the explosion, about four hundred letters from across Canada and the United States were sent to Halifax with offers to adopt these orphans.

In addition to the many injured children, there were lots of adults and soldiers at Halifax's Camp Hill Hospital. Soldiers were recovering from their war injuries, but they gave up their beds for those more seriously wounded from the explosion. The soldiers also got to work cleaning up the broken glass throughout the

Help Arrives

Ashpan Annie

Anne Liggins miraculously survived the Halifax Explosion. She was later given the nickname Ashpan Annie because it was ashes from a wood stove that helped keep her warm after the blast. At the time she was very young, not quite two years old. Her brother,

Ashpan Annie as a young child

Edwin, and her mother, Anne, were killed in the blast, which destroyed most of their house in Halifax's North End. The force of the explosion blew little Anne under the kitchen stove. The warm ashes in the ashpan underneath the stove kept her warm and alive for the next twenty-six hours until a soldier, his dog, and a neighbour discovered her. They took her to a hospital where she was later reunited with her grandmother and aunt. She lived until age ninety-five and died in Halifax in 2010.

hospital. Like the rest of the city, Camp Hill's windows had been shattered and had to be covered with boards to prevent the cold December air from entering the building. The wounded soldiers also helped carry in the wounded and lay them on mattresses on the hospital floor because there weren't enough beds for everyone.

At the Camp Hill Hospital, more than 1,400 injured people were crammed into a space meant to hold fewer than 250. There were many dead bodies too. They were brought to the hospital because no one knew where else

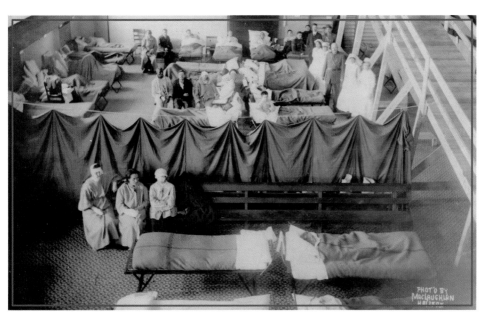

Many of the beds in Halifax hospitals were occupied by injured children.

to bring them. About 250 bodies were never identified, and many of those killed were never found.

When Barbara arrived at the hospital, she was taken inside on a stretcher. She was confused by what she saw: "I realized that there was something funny about the people. Most of them were dead," she later said. She lay quietly alone on her stretcher in the hallway. She didn't speak to anyone for a long time. Eventually she asked a man who worked in the hospital if she could get a bed.

Because she had been lying so still, the man had assumed she was dead. "I thought they were all beyond hope," he told her. He took her to a ward where staff cleaned and bandaged her crushed foot and leg. Then they left her.

Over the next few days in the hospital Barbara felt very lonely. More alone than she had ever felt in her life. She was scared. She didn't know anyone at the hospital, but most of all she didn't know where her family was. She missed them so much it hurt.

But she didn't give up hope.

"I don't think I had anything to eat," she later remembered of those first few days in the hospital. "I couldn't walk anyways. I hopped when I did get going. Nobody paid any attention. I just laid there and hoped

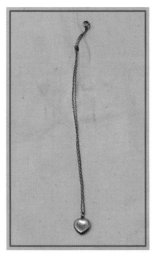

A locket from a girl who was probably a student at Richmond School with Barbara. The girl was never found.

that somebody would come. That's just the way you went. You'd see these streams of people going by, looking for people. I thought, well I don't know who will come, but maybe somebody."

Barbara wasn't the only lost child. In the chaos following the blast, hundreds of children became separated from their parents. Some were in hospitals like Barbara and others were at special homes for

Broken Pieces

children. All over the city, parents and families searched desperately for the ones they had lost. A few days after the explosion this ad ran in a Halifax newspaper:

"Ten-year-old, light brown hair, brown eyes, slender build, may have worn thick velvet cap, blue coat, ring on third finger with one stone. Missing since the explosion; her mother, who is in hospital, [is]very anxious for information."

The missing girl's brother, Charles, had placed the ad. It was printed many times over the next few months, but sadly it was never answered.

BLIZZARD

The day after the explosion it started to snow. As the day went on, the snow fell harder and brought with it freezing temperatures and blowing winds. Soon it was a full-blown blizzard and everything in Halifax was covered in snow. Some snowdrifts were as high as an adult's waist. The wind and snow blew right inside the homes and buildings that had been temporarily repaired.

Rescue workers had a difficult time digging out what lay underneath the wet, thick snow. In total, forty centimetres of snow was reported to have fallen on the city that day. Not only was the snow piled high, but where it met the heat from the burning buildings it turned into water and then ice. Before long, much of the wreckage was covered in ice, making rescue work almost impossible. Some survivors remained trapped inside frozen buildings and homes and died.

The storm and freezing-cold weather made life even harder for the more than six thousand people who were suddenly homeless. Public buildings, such as the Salvation Army barracks, the Majestic Theatre, and the Knights of Columbus Hall, were opened to allow families to stay there temporarily and to be sheltered from the terribly cold temperatures. Military tents were even set up on the Halifax Common to offer the homeless a little shelter from the wind and snow.

The blizzard raging throughout Nova Scotia and New Brunswick also slowed down trains that were carrying relief supplies to Halifax, or stopped them on the tracks. Deliveries of food and blankets became more and more difficult as the storm continued. The snow stopped finally on December 8.

Broken Pieces

Private Donald Angus Morrison of the 63rd Halifax Rifles shared his recollections after the explosion:

"I was walking up a street with a companion and we stopped to look at a building that had crumbled to the ground. I thought I heard someone crying. We poked around in the ruins and eventually found an opening to the cellar. There were no steps and we had no light. I told my friend that if he would hold me by the feet I would reach as far as I could and see what I would find. At first he didn't want to but he finally consented. I managed to reach the bottom on the cellar with my hands. We couldn't hear a sound and I thought perhaps I had imagined that cry when suddenly I felt some cloth and then something warm. I moved a board and it moved and whimpered—it was a small child. We managed to get her up—it was a little girl, badly bruised and frightened but alive. She told us she had gone to the cellar to feed her pussy cat before she went to school."

After ten lonely days in the hospital, Barbara was surprised to look up from her bed and see her aunt. From her bed, Barbara excitedly called out to her.

"Who are you?" her aunt asked, confused.

"It's me, Barbara!" She was shocked her aunt didn't recognize her.

"You can't be Barbara," replied her aunt. "Barbara has red hair." The soot and chemicals from the explosion had blackened Barbara's hair, and she also had cuts on her face and body that made her look different.

Eventually, Barbara's aunt recognized her niece and took Barbara home with her to Dartmouth. For the next few weeks, Barbara lived with her aunt and uncle. They had no children and took good care of her. They helped her recover. In her heart, Barbara believed her mother, father, and siblings had been killed in the explosion. But she hadn't given up all hope of finding them.

HELP FROM AROUND THE WORLD

While Barbara recovered, ships full of supplies kept arriving in Halifax Harbour. One ship from Boston brought glass to help replace the windows of the more than twelve thousand houses that had been damaged. Another ship came carrying

On December 17, 1917, a funeral march is played at a burial. Many unidentified bodies were found. They were buried at this ceremony, held in the Chebucto Road schoolyard.

Broken Pieces

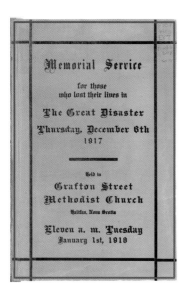

A notice for a memorial service held on January 1, 1918, for the victims of the explosion.

ten trucks. Trucks were needed to transport food and building materials to people so they could start rebuilding their homes. They were also needed to transport injured people to hospital and to take the people who had died to the morgue, a place where dead bodies were kept until they could be buried. Building supplies like nails and cement, and more than one thousand cases of boots and shoes also came by ship.

Donations were sent to Halifax from all across Canada, the United States, and Britain to help the city recover. The British government sent $5 million. A week after the explosion, the *Morning Chronicle* newspaper in Halifax printed a message sent from Buckingham Palace in London, England. King George wrote:

"Most deeply regret to hear of serious explosion at Halifax resulting in great loss of life and property. Please convey to Halifax, where I have spent so many happy times, my true sympathy in this grievous calamity."

People around the world read about the explosion in newspapers or heard about it on the radio and wanted to help. Some people sent $5, some $5,000. In 1917, $5 was a lot of money, considering $26 a week was good pay. In Windsor, Ontario, the #1 Girl Guides raised $2.50 to help. Children from British Guiana, on the northern coast of South America, raised $211.70.

CHRISTMAS 1917

Christmas was getting closer. Many people, like Barbara, did not feel like celebrating the holiday. But some who had survived the explosion were grateful to be alive and wanted to help others, especially the children who had lost family members. They saw Christmas as an opportunity to bring a little happiness to those who had suffered so much. Gifts came from Red Cross societies and church groups. The Massachusetts Relief Committee sent three hundred bags of toys to Halifax. Children who were in hospital or at orphanages were given toys, cake, and candy.

Some stores strung tinsel and hung ornaments. They tried to celebrate the season even though they still had boards covering their broken windows. But many people

A children's Christmas party held in December 1917.

didn't feel right about celebrating. Much of the city was in rubble. The fires were no longer burning, but funerals were still being held and dead bodies still being found amongst the fallen buildings. It was a sad time.

One nine-year-old girl from Halifax was kind enough to write to Santa Claus; she wanted to make sure he was okay.

Dear Santa Claus,
I hope you escaped all explosions and are safe. I
wish you a Merry Christmas.
Your friend,
Juanita Mallison

Collapsed buildings of Nova Scotia Car Works on Clifton Street in Halifax, 1918.

CHAPTER 5:

Finding Answers and Rebuilding the City

Barbara grew stronger every day, but for several months after the explosion she couldn't walk. As her strength slowly returned, she had to face the terrible truth she had hoped was only a bad dream: her family was gone. Every one of them had been killed in the explosion. She had known deep down that this was the truth, but hearing it from her uncle William was painful.

She missed her family, especially at night. When she lay alone in bed, she would let herself dream that she was back in her white house on Kenny Street with her mother and father and brothers and sisters. The dreams made her feel happy, but also deeply sad. She knew she would never see them again. She didn't know it then, but the pain of those dreams would fade as she got older.

Almost everything Barbara owned was lost, broken, or destroyed in the explosion. She held on tightly to her two remaining possessions: a piece of broken china from her house and a school picture of her brother Ian and her sister Mary.

TEMPORARY HOME IN TRURO

As Barbara's health improved, she had a difficult decision to make. Her uncle William asked if she wanted to continue living with her aunt and uncle in Dartmouth or come live with his family in Truro, a town about an hour's drive from Halifax. While she loved her relatives in Dartmouth, they lived alone and had no children. Her uncle William, who had worked at the Richmond Printing Company with her father, had two children. Barbara decided to move. Having grown up in a large family, she was used to having other children around.

Barbara moved to Truro with her aunt and uncle William and their two children. Like several other families who had lived in Richmond and had their homes destroyed, the family was living in Truro until they could build a new house and move back to Halifax.

Barbara and her two cousins went to school in Truro for several months before moving back to Halifax.

Once back in the city, the family moved into a bigger house on Windsor Street because Barbara's aunt's mother and father also decided to live with them. By now, there were seven people in the house and Barbara finally began to feel at home. She was growing closer to her new family. In many ways, they were like her old big family.

The love she received from her new family made her stronger and gave her the courage to not give up when she was sad or frustrated by her injuries. "They [the doctors] told me when they finally saw my ankle, that I'd never take part in sports again, and I'd never do this and that and the other thing," she said. "I can't do very much, but the one thing I could do was dance. I've got balance that

After the explosion, sledding wasn't just for fun. Children used sleds to haul supplies from a relief station to their families.

Finding Answers and Rebuilding the City

you wouldn't believe. I've done figure skating, played tennis—every game—soccer.... [But] for a long time, I'd walk along...I'd almost fall. It [eventually] got better."

CAUSE OF THE EXPLOSION

While Barbara got better with her new family, an investigation took place in Halifax to find out why and how the explosion had happened. Judges, lawyers, and more than fifty witnesses gathered for an **inquiry** led by Justice Arthur Drysdale.

Survivors of the explosion wait for food outside the Halifax Armoury in December 1917. Many people didn't have money to buy food after the explosion and many stores didn't have food to sell.

Broken Pieces

Initially unaware of what caused the explosion, many people in Halifax feared it was the Germans who had attacked the boats and made them explode. Because of this belief, German residents of Halifax were temporarily imprisoned and some even had insults and stones thrown at them. After the Halifax Explosion, German sailors captured at sea or those the Canadian government feared were dangerous were moved from the prison camp on Melville Island—located in the Halifax Harbour—to another camp in the town of Amherst, about two hours north.

The *Imo*'s Captain From died in the explosion, but the *Mont Blanc*'s Captain Le Medec survived. And he was hated. People were very angry with him because he had abandoned his ship. They thought he hadn't done enough to warn people of his vessel's dangerous cargo. They wanted to blame someone for the tragedy and since it wasn't the Germans, they turned their anger toward him. After the explosion, Captain Le Medec had to have police follow and protect him because he feared someone would try to hurt him.

Finding Answers and Rebuilding the City

THE VERDICT

On February 4, 1918, the man in charge of the inquiry, Judge Drysdale, delivered his findings. He found Captain Le Medec and Pilot Francis Mackey, whose job it was to guide ships safely in and out of the harbour, and Frederick Wyatt, the naval commanding officer in charge of the harbour at the time, guilty. He charged them with **manslaughter** and they were released on bail (meaning they leave jail after a certain amount of money was paid).

At the time, many people thought Captain Le Medec ignored Pilot Mackey's instructions and that Pilot Mackey had failed to notice that the ships were on a collision course and react quickly enough in the minutes before the explosion.

The criminal charges were later dropped. The court could not prove **gross negligence** causing death.

Later, the court decided Pilot Mackey had done everything he could, and it was not fair to blame him for the miscommunication between the boats. The blame was lifted and he was allowed to return to his job as a harbour pilot. The *Mont Blanc* was found solely to blame because the ship had been in the wrong place in

Broken Pieces

the channel and had cut in front of the *Imo*. The owners of the *Mont Blanc* fought this decision and the case went to Canada's highest court, the Supreme Court of Canada. There, a judge decided that both the *Imo* and the *Mont Blanc* were equally at fault. Finally, the Privy Council in London, England, gave the same verdict. (In 1918, people in Canada could appeal to the Privy Council as the last resort and "ultimate authority" for a decision.)

The city was being rebuilt while people tried to lay blame and punish those involved in the explosion. Docks, sheds, rail lines, and factories were repaired and plans were drawn for new wharves, schools, and houses. People were still hurt and struggling, but the Halifax waterfront would be rebuilt better than it was before.

THE HALIFAX RELIEF COMMISSION

On January 22, 1918, the Canadian government created the Halifax Relief Commission, which took over the work of the volunteer Halifax Relief Committee. Besides giving compensation, and medical and social services,

Finding Answers and Rebuilding the City

the commission built temporary housing and developed a master plan to rebuild the North End. The Halifax Relief Commission coordinated long-term relief efforts and remained in operation for almost sixty years, until 1976.

The commission had money to give families if a mother or father had been killed in the explosion. This money was called a **pension**. It provided some help for families that had lost their source of income. A widow received a monthly payment based on her family's income before the explosion. The payments were small—between $40 and $65 per month. If a family had a monthly income of $110 or less before the explosion, for example, the commission would pay the widow $40 a month, which was less than half of what the family was used to.

Halifax Relief Committee

The Halifax Relief Committee (as opposed to Commission) was a volunteer organization which was organized within hours of the explosion to coordinate relief efforts. It worked to find shelter for the homeless, identify the dead and injured, construct temporary housing, and determine which buildings had been damaged and destroyed.

Broken Pieces

The Halifax Relief Commission organized temporary housing in Halifax's North End. By mid-March 1918, three months after the explosion, forty new two-storey buildings were home to more than two thousand people. The apartments were furnished with beds and chairs and tables donated by the Massachusetts-Halifax Relief Committee, a local committee which oversaw how the relief money from Massachusetts would be distributed in Halifax.

Work also started right away to restore churches in the city. Religion played a central role in people's lives in 1917 and the restoration of churches was seen as just as important as building schools and businesses. Many people felt that churches were necessary not only to worship God, but for sustaining faith and courage through such a difficult time. They were places where communities came together to support one another.

THE HYDROSTONE NEIGHBOURHOOD

In September 1918, work got underway to redesign a large portion of the North End. The Halifax Relief Commission hired urban planner Thomas Adams

JOB
1918

71

Shown here is the Hydrostone, a new neighbourhood that would be built in Richmond.

to design and build a whole new neighbourhood and replace the homes that had been flattened in the blast. Thomas Adams was inspired by a concept known as the "garden city." The idea was to have a neighbourhood filled with nice-looking houses, nearby parks and open spaces, stores, and improved roads. This new neighbourhood became known as "the Hydrostone" and was the first planned urban community in Canada.

Broken Pieces

The name came from the main building material used to construct the new homes and stores. Instead of wood, Adams thought large concrete blocks would be more durable if there were ever another explosion. The blocks of stone were made in Eastern Passage, outside Dartmouth, and a special railway line was constructed to transport the material from the docks to the North End.

100 Men
WANTED

WANTED at Eastern Passage, 100 handy men for Hydorstone Making. Best wages paid. First class board on the job. Apply at works Plant Wharf, or 159 Upper Water Street.

THE NOVA SCOTIA CONSTRUC-TION CO., LTD.

3551 hm t f.

Newspaper clipping calling for workers to make hydrostones. Taken from *The Halifax Herald* August 26, 1918, p.9.

In 1918, people knew more about construction and built their new homes so that they were stronger and safer. Building materials had greatly improved. These concrete blocks were fire resistant, whereas the homes before the explosion were mostly built with wood.

The first twenty-four homes in the Hydrostone district were ready by March 1919. They were built quickly, with twenty more to be finished every two weeks. The whole neighbourhood was completed by 1922. Soon some two

Men make the hydrostone blocks in 1919 at the Canadian Hydro-Stone Plant in Eastern Passage, Nova Scotia.

thousand people were living there. Monthly rent ranged from $25 for a four-room apartment to $50 for a seven-room house.

On February 10, 1921, the *Evening Echo* newspaper printed essays written by students of Alexander McKay School and Richmond School who now lived in the Hydrostone: "I like my new home. I am not afraid of the fire in the night there. The streets are cement…there are dry goods and groceries and drug

Broken Pieces

These houses in Halifax's North End were built by the Halifax Relief Commission's Reconstruction Department.

stores. The houses are nice inside," wrote a boy who had lost his home, his father, and his brother in the explosion.

BACK TO SCHOOL

It was May 1918—five months after the explosion—before children in Richmond returned to school, and

Finding Answers and Rebuilding the City

Barbara Orr and her class at the Ladies' College. Barbara is in the front row, in the middle.

even then it was only part-time. School was much different now. The Richmond School students went for half a day to Alexander McKay School because their school had to be rebuilt, but many of their classmates were not there. Some had been killed, others had moved away. Almost everyone had signs of injuries and many had spent time in the hospital. All the children in Richmond had been in great danger and most of them had lost close relatives or friends. They also now lived in different homes. Little, if anything, was the same.

Broken Pieces

Since Barbara now lived in a different area of the city with her uncle William and his family, she went to a different school called the Halifax Ladies' College. At first, she didn't like her new school, but with time she did.

At school, Barbara spent as much time as she could making art. She loved art and would continue to paint in watercolours and make art throughout her life. When her leg healed, she went back to playing sports too, something the doctors told her she would never be able to do. She loved to figure skate and she was very good at it. All of these interests helped her to keep busy and to make her happy again. But she always remembered her family and was often sad that they were no longer in her life.

As she grew closer to her uncle and her new family, Barbara began to feel a sense of belonging once again, which made her sadness less painful. Being a big family, they reminded her of her parents and siblings. "My uncle was a wonderful man. [They were] a wonderful family to grow up with," Barbara later recalled.

Barbara was very creative and loved painting with watercolours, like she did with this piece.

CHAPTER 6:

Remembrance and Lessons for the Future

MEANINGFUL CHURCH BELLS

*F*our years after the explosion, in 1921, the United Memorial Church in Richmond held a special service. The church had been rebuilt to replace the neighbourhood's two churches that were destroyed in the explosion. Barbara was asked to play a hymn on the church bells.

The bells had special meaning for Barbara. Her uncle William had donated them to the church, and they hung in the church's tower in memory of Barbara's family. The names of her mother, father, and siblings were etched into the largest bell.

When the day of the service arrived, Barbara was nervous. "Suppose I make a mistake," she said at the time.

Remembrance and Lessons for the Future

"It will be heard as far away as Dartmouth." But she took a deep breath, thought of her family, and didn't make a mistake. The loud, clear sound travelled across the area that had been destroyed in the explosion four years earlier. When the bells tolled, those who could hear them paused and remembered.

The simple, melodic notes were a sad reminder of the loss both the city and Barbara had endured. But they were also a signal of rebirth. The area was being rebuilt, the survivors had started new lives filled with hope, and life was continuing on.

MEMORIAL BELL TOWER

For more than forty years the heavy bells hung in the United Memorial Church. They eventually had to be taken down when the church tower cracked, no longer able to support their weight and vibrations. For eight years the bells lay covered in tarp on the church lawn, awaiting their new home. When a group called the Halifax Explosion Memorial Bells Committee formed in 1983, it began plans to build a bell tower on the top of Fort Needham to keep alive the memory of those

Broken Pieces

who had died or been injured in the explosion. A new home was finally found for the bells.

On June 9, 1985, a special ceremony was held to dedicate the Memorial Bell Tower to the people who were killed or injured in the explosion. Barbara was there once again

Barbara and her cousin Bill at the dedication ceremony for the bells at Fort Needham in 1985.

to play the bells. She was married now and had one daughter of her own. She named her only child Barbara. At this ceremony, her cousin Bill helped her play the bells. While she played, her thoughts likely went back to the cold winter day sixty-eight years earlier when the explosion's force had thrown her through the air and landed her near the spot where the memorial tower and bells now stood.

The bells called Barbara and the other survivors who had gathered for the dedication ceremony to once again stop and remember those who had died in 1917.

Remembrance and Lessons for the Future

Some asked themselves a question they had thought of often over the years. Why were *they* the lucky ones to survive, while so many others had been killed? They couldn't easily find an answer. Survivors of tragedies are often left with a mixture of sadness, guilt, and gratitude. They experience these feelings all their lives. Survivors also often feel a strong duty to keep the memory of those who died alive to make certain that they are never forgotten.

A SAD ANNIVERSARY

Every year at 9:05 A.M. on December 6, a service is held at the bell tower at Fort Needham in memory of the victims of the Halifax Explosion. Across the Narrows and all through the areas devastated by the explosion, the bells ring out. A moment of silence is held, just like on Remembrance Day, to remember the tragedy and all those who lost their lives.

Even though the Halifax Explosion occurred one hundred years ago, people haven't forgotten. Stories of the explosion and the people affected continue to be shared worldwide. Those stories will only be forgotten when they stop being shared. Nearly all of the people who lived

Broken Pieces

through the explosion are no longer alive. But their stories live on through their great-grandchildren, and through teachers and other storytellers. Inside libraries and at the Nova Scotia Archives in Halifax there are many more stories waiting to be discovered.

REMEMBERING THE EXPLOSION

In 1917, there were no television cameras to record the Halifax Explosion, so people mostly relied on newspapers to get their news. Film did exist, however. Today, moving images of the Halifax Explosion can still be viewed. On the Nova Scotia Archives website you can watch thirteen minutes of black-and-white moving images taken by a professional cameraman named W. G. MacLaughlan. The film is silent because in the early days of film, cameras were only able to capture images, not sound. Watching the black-and-white images of the destruction in silence conveys the strange and frightening feeling everyone had in the aftermath of the explosion. See page 97 for the link.

Another way the explosion is remembered is through books. Twenty-four years after the explosion, Halifax writer Hugh MacLennan wrote his first novel, *Barometer Rising*.

Remembrance and Lessons for the Future

The popular 1941 book is set during and after the Halifax Explosion. In the book, Penelope Wain believes that the man she loves, Neil Macrae, has been killed while serving overseas during the First World War. What she doesn't know is that Neil is not dead, but has returned to Halifax.

Michael Bird's 1962 non-fiction book *The Town That Died* is a moving and detailed chronicle of the tragic events that took place after the explosion. It tells the personal experiences of those who were there.

In the late 1980s, Janet Kitz, a Halifax researcher and author, interviewed more survivors of the explosion and pored over artifacts at the public archives to uncover new information and stories. Before her research and interviews, people who lived through the explosion had mostly wanted to forget those memories and rarely talked about the disaster. Her research sparked a new interest in the explosion.

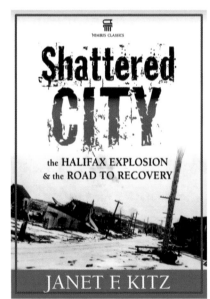

The cover of Janet Kitz's popular book, *Shattered City: The Halifax Explosion and The Road to Recovery.*

Broken Pieces

In 1989, Kitz published a book called *Shattered City: The Halifax Explosion and the Road to Recovery*. A television miniseries based on the book aired on CBC in 2003, called *Shattered City: The Halifax Explosion*. In 1992, Kitz wrote another book about the explosion that focused on children. It is called *Survivors: Children of the Halifax Explosion*. She also created slide presentations on the Halifax Explosion for both schoolchildren and adults. Over the years, she has given many talks and lectures based on aspects of the explosion. Her books have inspired many people to do further research.

MARITIME MUSEUM OF THE ATLANTIC

Inside the Maritime Museum of the Atlantic on Halifax's waterfront, there is a permanent explosion-related exhibit called *Halifax Wrecked*. It has photographs and artifacts from the explosion, such as pencils and erasers found in the school desks of students after the explosion, and railway dispatcher Vincent Coleman's watch. Several pieces of metal that flew across the city from the *Mont Blanc* are part of the collection too.

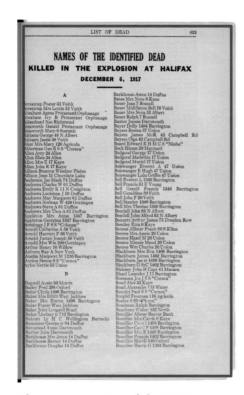

NAMES OF THE IDENTIFIED DEAD
KILLED IN THE EXPLOSION AT HALIFAX
DECEMBER 6, 1917

The paper version of the 2002 *Remembrance Book* includes the names of identified victims, their ages, and where they were buried. The master copy is on permanent display at the Maritime Museum of the Atlantic in Halifax.

Also at the Maritime Museum of the Atlantic is *The Halifax Explosion Remembrance Book*. This book is a record of the men, women, and children known to have died on December 6, 1917, or in the days or months following as a direct result of the explosion. The *Remembrance Book* is now an online database that has 1,946 names, which you can search through on the Nova Scotia Archives website.

Throughout Halifax's North End, traces of the explosion can still be found. The houses and schools built after the explosion remain standing today. Since the houses were built using hydrostone, they have lasted much longer than some of the wooden homes around the city.

Broken Pieces

LESSONS LEARNED

After the explosion and the inquiry that followed, the rules about how ships could enter and exit Halifax Harbour became clearer and easier to follow. The inquiry found that the explosion could have been avoided altogether. With so many explosives on-board, the *Mont Blanc* should never have entered a harbour surrounded by a city.

Looking back, one of the most important and lasting lessons to take from the explosion is the importance of kindness in the hours and days after the disaster. Years later, survivors often spoke about the compassion, generosity, and hospitality of strangers. In a time of despair, people came together to help those who needed it most.

Fire Fighters' Monument

On December 6, 1992, firefighters in Halifax dedicated a three-metre monument made of black polished granite to their colleagues who died in the explosion. It is outside Station 4 in the city's North End. These brave firefighters died responding to the fires around the city with their new fire engine called the *Patricia*.

The three-metre Fire Fighters' Monument.

BOSTON CHRISTMAS TREE

As a way to say "thank you" for the medical supplies, doctors, and money Boston sent Halifax after the explosion, each year a special Christmas tree grown in Nova Scotia is sent to the American city. A perfect spruce tree, standing at least fifteen metres tall with flawless branches. In Boston, the tree is decorated with thousands of lights and shines in the centre of the city as a reminder of Nova Scotians' gratitude for the aid Boston so generously sent.

A Christmas tree is sent to Boston every year, as a thank you from the people of Halifax.

Broken Pieces

ONE HUNDRED YEARS LATER

One hundred years later, the story of the explosion is no less sad because so much time has passed. It remains Halifax's story of devastation and despair, but it is also a tale of recovery, hope, and learning from past mistakes.

By learning about the stories of people like Barbara Orr, who lived through the devastation, and Vincent Coleman, who died trying to save others, we can see these heroes as real people, and connect with them.

We also make sure they are never forgotten.

Remembrance and Lessons for the Future

Acknowledgments

First I would like to say thank you to everyone at Nimbus Publishing, in particular Whitney Moran, Emily MacKinnon, Jenn Embree and Lexi Harrington.

My gratitude to all those who wrote about the Halifax Explosion before me, especially Janet Kitz, Michael Bird, Alan Ruffman, and Colin D. Howell. Their research and insight were invaluable. Sally Walker's *Blizzard of Glass: The Halifax Explosion of 1917* was similarly inspirational. It showed me what a good children's book about the Explosion could be like.

Thanks are also due to the Nova Scotia Archives, the Maritime Museum of the Atlantic, CBC, Halifax Regional Municipality, the Halifax Public Libraries, and Heather Huggard for their wonderful collections of books, newspapers, photographs, and other material.

Finally, my deepest thanks to my family—Robbie, Natasha, and Lara. Learning about Barbara Orr's story was a poignant reminder of how lonely life would be without you.

Glossary

Benzene: A highly flammable fuel. It is still used today in gasoline. The benzene on-board the *Mont Blanc* was destined for military aircraft at war in France.

Bow: The front of a boat.

Convoy: During the First World War, ships crossed the Atlantic Ocean together in groups known as convoys. The ships would protect each other from attacks by German submarines.

Enlisted: Signed up to go to war.

Gross Negligence: the legal term to describe when there is a knowing lack of care or caution and the consequences of that are serious to the safety or property of another person.

Guncotton: An explosive. When it is dry, it turns into a white fluffy substance that looks like cotton.

Inquiry: an official investigation into something.

Manslaughter: the legal term for killing someone without planning it beforehand.

Pension: A set amount of money that is paid regularly. After the explosion, it was paid to families to allow them to pay bills and buy food.

Picric Acid: An extremely dangerous chemical. It is still used today as an ingredient in explosives, laboratories, and to make dye and fertilizer.

Port: The left-hand side of the ship when facing forward.

S. S.: The initials before the name of a ship stand for Steam Ship, before motorized ships (M. S.) became the norm. A steamship is a ship that is driven or moved by a steam engine.

Starboard: The right-hand side of a ship when facing forward.

Stern: The back of a boat.

Telegram: A written message sent using an electric device. The message was carried along wires, and the text written or printed and delivered by hand or teleprinter. In 1917, telegrams were used often, because private telephones were not common.

TNT: An explosive that creates a high-pressure blast. The United States military continues to use it today.

Tsunami: A Japanese word that translates into English as "harbour wave." It is a series of large waves *caused* by an earthquake, underwater volcanic eruption, landslide, or some other sudden ocean disturbance (such as the Halifax Explosion).

Timeline

1917

December 1 – The French ship *Mont Blanc* leaves New York City on its way to Halifax. In New York, the ship had been loaded with a mixture of explosives and fuel.

December 5 – The *Mont Blanc* arrives at Halifax Harbour to find the gates of the submarine nets are closed until morning. The *Mont Blanc* anchors near McNabs Island.

December 5 – The Belgian relief ship *Imo* is anchored inside Bedford Basin. It plans to leave the next day for New York.

December 6, 7:30 A.M. – The submarine nets are opened and the *Mont Blanc* enters the harbour.

December 6, 8:45 A.M. – *Imo* collides with *Mont Blanc* in the Narrows. A fire starts aboard the *Mont Blanc*.

December 6, at precisely 09:04:35 A.M. – The *Mont Blanc* explodes. The explosion causes a tsunami in the harbour.

December 7 – A blizzard hits Halifax, making it difficult for rescue workers to find survivors. The snow stops trains from delivering relief supplies.

December 13 – An inquiry begins to find out what caused the explosion and who is to blame. Justice Arthur Drysdale hears testimony from more than fifty witnesses.

1918

January 22 – The Halifax Relief Commission is appointed by the Canadian government. Widows, orphans, and those who suffered serious permanent injuries are given pensions or a lump sum of money.

February 4 – Justice Drysdale decides the *Mont Blanc* was solely at fault for the disaster. But the Supreme Court of Canada later finds that both the *Mont Blanc* and the *Imo* were equally at fault.

1985

June 9 – The Halifax Explosion Memorial Bell Tower on Fort Needham is dedicated to those affected by the explosion. It also honours the survivors who rebuilt Halifax and Dartmouth.

2017

December 6 – Marks the one-hundredth anniversary of the Halifax Explosion.

Resources

CHILDREN'S BOOKS

Halsey, Jacqueline and Loretta Migani. *Explosion Newsie.* Halifax: Formac Publishing Company, 2015.

Lawson, Julie. *Dear Canada: No Safe Harbour: The Halifax Explosion Diary of Charlotte Blackburn.* Toronto: Scholastic Canada, 2006.

Lawson, Julie. *A Blinding Light.* Halifax: Nimbus Publishing, 2017.

Payzant, Joan. *Who's a Scaredy-Cat! A Story of the Halifax Explosion.* Halifax: Nimbus Publishing, 2005.

Walker, Sally M. *Blizzard of Glass: The Halifax Explosion of 1917.* New York: Henry Holt and Company, 2011.

GENERAL BOOKS

Armstrong, John Griffith. *The Halifax Explosion and the Royal Canadian Navy.* Vancouver: UBC Press, 2002.

Beed, Blair. *1917 Halifax Explosion and American Response.* Halifax: Nimbus Publishing, 2010.

Bird, Michael J. *The Town That Died: A Chronicle of the Halifax Explosion.* Halifax: Nimbus Publishing, 1995, 2011.

Bird, Will. *This is Nova Scotia.* Toronto: The Ryerson Press, 1950.

Chapman, Harry. *Dartmouth's Day of Anguish.* Dartmouth: The Dartmouth Historical Association, 1992.

Erickson, Paul. *Historic North End Halifax.* Halifax: Nimbus Publishing, 2004.

Flemming, David. *Explosion in Halifax Harbour: The Illustrated Account of a Disaster that Shook the World.* Halifax: Formac Publishing Company, 2004.

Glasner, Joyce. *The Halifax Explosion: Surviving the Blast that Shook a Nation.* Canmore: Altitude Publishing, 2003.

Glasner, Joyce. *The Halifax Explosion: Heroes and Survivors.* Toronto: James Lorimer & Company Ltd., 2011.

Hebert Boyd, Michelle. *Enriched by Catastrophe: Social Work and Social Conflict After the Halifax Explosion.* Halifax: Fernwood Publishing, 2007.

Kelly, Gemey. *Arthur Lismer: Nova Scotia, 1916–1919.* Halifax: Dalhousie Art Gallery, 1982.

Kitz, Janet. *Shattered City: The Halifax Explosion and the Road to Recovery.* Halifax: Nimbus Publishing, 1989.

Kitz, Janet. *Survivors: Children of the Halifax Explosion.* Halifax: Nimbus Publishing, 1992.

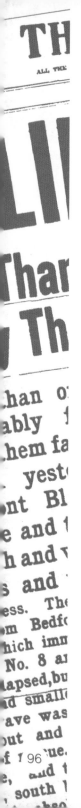

Kitz, Janet and Payzant, Joan. *December 1917: Re-Visiting the Halifax Explosion.* Halifax: Nimbus Publishing, 2006.

MacLennan, Hugh. *Barometer Rising.* Toronto: Penguin, Random House Canada, 2007.

Mahar, James and Mahar, Rowena. *Too Many to Mourn.* Halifax: Nimbus Publishing, 1998.

Maybee, Janet. *Aftershock: The Halifax Explosion and the Persecution of Pilot Francis Mackey.* Halifax: Nimbus Publishing, 2015.

Metson, Graham. *The Halifax Explosion December 6, 1917.* Toronto: McGraw-Hill Ryerson Ltd., 1978.

Monnon, Mary Ann. *Miracles and Mysteries: The Halifax Explosion.* Halifax: Nimbus Publishing, 1977.

WEBSITES

Halifax Explosion 100 Years 100 Stories: 100years100stories.ca/

CBC Halifax Explosion Site: cbc.ca/halifaxexplosion

Halifax Regional Municipality: halifax.ca/halifaxexplosion/history.php

Maritime Museum of the Atlantic: maritimemuseum.novascotia.ca/what-see-do/halifax-explosion

Nova Scotia Archives: novascotia.ca/archives/virtual

Index

Index

Image Credits

Nova Scotia Archives: iv (bottom), 2, 8, 11, 12, 17, 18, 20, 26, 28, 35, 37, 40, 42, 44, 53, 59, 62, 65, 66, 72, 73, 74, 75, 86

Maritime Museum of the Atlantic: iv (top), 36, 47, 52, 54

Janet Kitz's personal collection: 5, 76

Family of Barbara Orr Thompson: cover, 78, 81

City of Toronto Archives: 58, 61

Dartmouth Heritage Museum: 13

Len Wagg: 88

Courtesy of the Nova Scotia Museum, Halifax, Nova Scotia, Photographed by Adam Hartling, NSM #Z3887: 39

Courtesy of the Maritime Museum of the Atlantic, Halifax, Nova Scotia, a part of the Nova Scotia Museum, National Archives, U.S.A., Print #165-ww-158A-15: 41